CONTENTS

INTRODUCTION

Where there is a smoke, there is a flavor. Smoking meat or making BBQ is not only a means of cooking but for some individuals and classy enthusiasts, this is a form of Art! Or dare I say a form of lifestyle! Enthusiasts all around the world have been experimenting and dissecting the secrets of perfectly smoked meat for decades now, and in our golden age, perhaps they have cracked it up completely!In our age, the technique of Barbequing or Smoking meat has been perfected to such a level, that a BBQ Grill is pretty much an essential amenity found in all backyard or sea-beach parties!

This is the drinking fountain for the more hip and adventurous people, who prefer to have a nice chat with their friends and families while smoking up a few batches of Burger Patty for them to enjoy. But here's the thing, while this art might seem as a very easy form of cooking which only requires you to flip meats over and over! Mastering it might be a little bit difficult if you don't know have the proper information with you. This guide is an essential book for beginners who want to smoke meat without needing expert help from others. This book offers detailed guidance obtained by years of smoking meat, includes clear instructions and step-by-step directions for every recipe. This is the only guide you will ever need to professionally smoke a variety of food. The book includes full-color photographs of every finished meal to make your job easier. Whether you are a beginner meat smoker or looking to go beyond the basics, the book gives you the tools and tips you need to start that perfectly smoked meat. Smoking is something has withstood the test of time, it will continue to stand the test of time for years to come. Not only is it a method to preserve your catch or kill, but it's also one of if not the best-tasting food there is.

CHAPTER-1 BEEF

BBQ Smoked Beef Brisket with Red Wine Marinade

(Cooking Time 6 Hours 10 Minutes)

Ingredients for 10 servings

- Beef Brisket (5-lb., 2.3-kg.)

The Marinade

- Red wine – 2 cups
- Olive oil – ¾ cup
- Mustard – 2 tablespoons
- Lemon juice – 2 tablespoons
- Wine vinegar – 1 ½ tablespoons
- Salt – 1 tablespoon
- Cayenne pepper – ½ teaspoon
- Onion powder – 1 ½ teaspoons
- Garlic powder – 1 ½ teaspoons

The Rub

- Brown sugar – ½ cup
- Salt – 1 teaspoon
- Black pepper – 2 teaspoons
- Smoked paprika – 2 teaspoons
- Garlic powder – 2 teaspoons
- Onion powder – 2 teaspoons
- Mustard – 1 ½ teaspoons
- Cayenne pepper – ½ teaspoon

The Liquid

- Water – 2 cups

The Heat

- Hickory wood chips, soak for an hour

Method

1.   Combine red wine with olive oil, mustard, lemon juice, wine vinegar, salt, cayenne pepper, onion powder, and garlic powder. Stir well.

2.   Season the brisket with the red wine mixture then marinade for overnight. Store in the fridge to keep it fresh.

3.   On the next day, remove the marinated brisket from the fridge and thaw at room temperature.

4.   Next, pour water into an iron pan then place in the gas smoker.

5.   Spread the soaked woodchips on the tray then set in the gas smoker as well.

6.   After that, ignite your gas smoker and get it ready. Let it reach 225°F (107°C).

7.   In the meantime, combine the rub ingredients—brown sugar, salt, black pepper, smoked paprika, garlic powder, onion powder, mustard, and cayenne pepper in a bowl then mix well.

8.   Rub the spice mixture over the brisket and once the gas smoker is ready, place the seasoned beef brisket in the smoker.

9.   Smoke the beef brisket for approximately 6 hours or until the internal temperature has reached 190°F (88°C).

10.   Remove the smoked beef brisket from the gas smoker and transfer to a serving dish.

11.   Serve and enjoy.

(Cooking Time 4 Hours 30 Minutes)

Ingredients for 10 servings

- Beef Ribs (3.5-lb., 1.6-kg.)

The Brine

- Water – 2 quarts
- Salt – 2 tablespoons
- Cayenne pepper – 1 tablespoon
- Brown sugar – 2 tablespoons
- Garlic powder – 1 tablespoon
- Cumin – ¾ tablespoon
- Dried basil – 1 teaspoon

The Rub

- Smoked paprika – 2 tablespoons
- White sugar – ¼ cup
- Brown sugar – 1 tablespoon
- Garlic powder – 2 tablespoons
- Onion powder – 1 tablespoon
- Chili powder – 1 tablespoon
- Salt – ½ tablespoon
- Cayenne pepper – 1 tablespoon
- Cumin – ¾ tablespoon
- Black pepper – 1 tablespoon
- Oregano – ½ tablespoon
- Dried thyme – ½ teaspoon

The Glaze

- Maple Syrup – 1 cup
- Olive oil – ¼ cup

The Liquid

- Apple juice – 2 cups

The Heat

- Hickory wood chips, soak for an hour

- Apple wood chips, soak for an hour

Method

1. Pour water into a container then season with salt, cayenne pepper, brown sugar, garlic powder, cumin, and dried basil. Stir until incorporated.

2. Add beef ribs to the brine mixture then soak for overnight. Store in the fridge to keep it fresh.

3. On the next day, remove the beef ribs from the fridge and take the ribs out of the brine. Wash and rinse the beef ribs then pat it dry.

4. Next, pour apple juice into an iron pan then place in the gas smoker.

5. Spread the mixed soaked woodchips on the tray then set in the gas smoker as well.

6. After that, ignite your gas smoker and get it ready. Let it reach 225°F (107°C).

7. Mix smoked paprika with white sugar; brown sugar, garlic powder, onion powder, chili powder, salt, cayenne pepper, cumin, black pepper, oregano, and dried thyme then rub over the beef ribs.

8. Once the gas smoker is ready, place the seasoned beef ribs in the smoker and smoke for approximately 4 hours.

9. In the meantime, combine maple syrup with olive oil then stir until incorporated.

10. Wait until the internal temperature of the smoked beef ribs reaches 185°F (85°C), then baste the maple syrup and olive oil mixture over the smoked beef ribs.

11. Continue smoking for about 30 minutes or until the smoked beef ribs have a shining appearance then remove from the gas smoker.

12. Transfer the smoked beef ribs to a serving dish then serve.

13. Enjoy!

(Cooking Time 6 Hours 10 Minutes)

Ingredients for 10 servings

- Beef Ribs (6-lb., 2.7-kg.)

The Spray

- Apple juice – ¼ cup
- Mustard – ½ tablespoon
- Maple syrup – 1 tablespoon

The Rub

- Brown sugar – 2 tablespoons
- Salt – 1 ½ tablespoons
- Black pepper – 1 teaspoon
- Smoked paprika – 1 teaspoon
- Garlic powder – 1 teaspoon
- Onion powder – 1 teaspoon
- Mustard – ½ teaspoon
- Cinnamon – 1 teaspoon
- Cayenne pepper – ½ teaspoon

The Glaze

- Ketchup – ¾ cup
- Yellow mustard – ½ cup
- Maple syrup – ½ cup
- White vinegar – 1 tablespoon
- Black pepper – 1 teaspoon

The Liquid

- Apple juice – 2 cups

The Heat

- Apple wood chips, soak for an hour

Method

1. Combine apple juice with mustard and maple syrup then stir until incorporated. Spray over the beef ribs.

2.   Next, place the entire rub ingredients—brown sugar, salt, black pepper, smoked paprika, garlic powder, onion powder, mustard, cinnamon, and cayenne pepper in a bowl then mix well.

3.   Rub the beef ribs with the spice mixture then let it rest for about an hour.

4.   In the meantime, pour apple juice into an iron pan then place in the gas smoker.

5.   Spread the soaked woodchips on the tray then set in the gas smoker as well.

6.   After that, ignite your gas smoker and get it ready. Let it reach 225°F (107°C).

7.   Once the gas smoker is ready, place the seasoned beef ribs in the smoker and smoke for 3 hours.

8.   After 3 hours of smoking, open the gas smoker then wrap the beef ribs with aluminum foil.

9.   Quickly return the wrapped beef ribs to the gas smoker and continue smoking for 2 hours.

10.   Meanwhile, combine ketchup with yellow mustard, maple syrup, white vinegar, and black pepper then stir until incorporated. Set aside.

11.   Wait until the internal temperature of the smoked beef ribs reaches 185°F (85°C) then unwrap the ribs.

12.   Glaze the smoked beef ribs with the ketchup and maple syrup mixture then return to the gas smoker. Smoke for an hour.

13.   Once it is done, remove the smoked beef ribs from the gas smoker and transfer to a serving dish.

14.   Serve and enjoy.

(Cooking Time 5 Hours 10 Minutes)
Ingredients for 10 servings
- Beef Brisket (4-lbs., 1.8-kg.)

The Marinade
- Worcestershire sauce – 3 tablespoons
- Apple cider vinegar – 2 tablespoons
- Yellow mustard – ¼ cup
- Whole grain mustard – 2 tablespoons
- Water – 2 tablespoons

The Rub
- Salt – 1 tablespoon
- Black pepper – 2 tablespoons
- Garlic powder – 2 tablespoons
- Onion powder – 2 tablespoons
- Lemon pepper – 1 tablespoon
- Chili powder – 1 tablespoon
- Cayenne powder – 1 teaspoon

The Glaze
- Honey – ¾ cup
- Bourbon – ¾ cup
- Brown sugar – ½ cup

The Liquid
- Water – 2 cups
- Lemon juice – 2 tablespoons

The Heat
- Hickory wood chips, soak for an hour

Method
1. Mix Worcestershire sauce with apple cider vinegar, yellow mustard, whole grain mustard, and water then stir well.
2. Rub the beef brisket with the spice mixture then marinate for overnight. Place in a container with a lid and store in the fridge to keep it fresh.

3.　　　On the next day, take the marinated beef brisket out of the fridge then thaw at room temperature.

4.　　　Next, pour water and lemon juice into an iron pan then place in the gas smoker.

5.　　　Spread the soaked woodchips on the tray then set in the gas smoker as well.

6.　　　After that, ignite your gas smoker and get it ready. Let it reach 225°F (107°C).

7.　　　In the meantime, combine the rub ingredients—salt, black pepper, garlic powder, onion powder, lemon pepper, chili powder, and cayenne pepper in a bowl then mix well.

8.　　　Apply the spice mixture over the beef brisket and once the gas smoker is ready, place the seasoned beef brisket in the smoker. Smoke the beef brisket for approximately 4 hours.

9.　　　While waiting for the smoked beef brisket, combine honey with bourbon and brown sugar then stir until incorporated. Set aside.

10.　　　After 4 hours of smoking, take the smoked beef out of the gas smoker then glaze with the honey-bourbon mixture.

11.　　　Wrap the glazed beef brisket and return to the gas smoker.

12.　　　Smoked the wrapped beef brisket for an hour then check the internal temperature.

13.　　　Wait until the internal temperature of the smoked beef brisket has reached 190°F (88°C) and remove from the gas smoker. Let it cool for a few minutes.

14.　　　Unwrap the smoked beef brisket then transfer to a serving dish.

15.　　　Serve and enjoy.

(Cooking Time 5 Hours 10 Minutes)

Ingredients for 10 servings

- Beef Brisket (5-lb., 2.3-kg.)

The Rub

- Brown sugar – 1 cup
- White sugar – 1 cup
- Smoked paprika – ¼ cup
- Garlic powder – 2 tablespoons
- Onion powder – 1 tablespoon
- Black pepper – 1 ½ tablespoons
- Ground ginger – 1 tablespoon
- Dried rosemary – 1 teaspoon

The Glaze

- Wine vinegar – 1 tablespoon
- Brown sugar – 3 tablespoons
- Orange juice – ¼ cup
- Honey – ¼ cup
- Ground clove – A pinch

The Sauce

- Diced red chilies – 2 tablespoons
- Ground ginger – ½ teaspoon
- Garlic powder – 1 teaspoon
- Diced red tomatoes – 2 cups
- Caster sugar – 1 cup
- Red wine vinegar – ¾ cup

The Liquid

- Water – 2 cups

The Heat

- Hickory wood chips, soak for an hour

Method

1.   Combine the rub ingredients—brown sugar, white sugar, smoked paprika, garlic powder, onion powder, black pepper, ground ginger, and dried rosemary in a bowl then mix well.

2.   Rub the beef brisket with the spice mixture then set aside.

3.   Next, pour water into an iron pan then place in the gas smoker.

4.   Spread the soaked woodchips on the tray then set in the gas smoker as well.

5.   After that, ignite your gas smoker and get it ready. Let it reach 225°F (107°C).

6.   Once the gas smoker is ready, place the seasoned beef brisket in the smoker and smoke for 3 hours.

7.   In the meantime, place the glaze ingredients—wine vinegar, brown sugar, orange juice, honey, and ground clove in a bowl then stir well.

8.   After 3 hours of smoking, brush the glaze mixture over the beef then wrap with aluminum foil.

9.   Return the wrapped beef to the smoker then smoke for another 2 hours or until the internal temperature of the smoked beef has reached 190°F (88°C).

10.   Once it is done, remove the smoked beef from the gas smoker and let it cool for a few minutes.

11.   Place red chilies, ground ginger, garlic powder, red tomatoes, and red wine vinegar to a food processor then process until smooth.

12.   Transfer the smooth mixture to a saucepan then bring to a simmer.

13.   Add caster sugar to the saucepan then stir until dissolved. Remove from heat.

14.   Unwrap the smoked beef then place on a serving dish.

15.   Drizzle the sauce over the smoked beef then serve.

16.   Enjoy!

CHAPTER-2 PORK

Raspberry Glazed Smoked Pork with Sweet Brown Rub

(Cooking Time 5 Hours 30 Minutes)

Ingredients for 10 servings

- Pork Ribs (6-lb., 2.7-kg.)

The Brine

- Water – 8 cups
- Salt – ½ cup
- White sugar – ¼ cup
- Brown sugar – 3 tablespoons
- Rosemary sprigs – 3
- Bay leaves – 2
- Chopped onion – ¼ cup
- Minced garlic – 2 tablespoons
- Smoked paprika – ¾ tablespoon
- Cayenne pepper – ¼ teaspoon

The Rub

- Brown sugar – ½ cup
- Salt – 1 ½ tablespoons
- Black pepper – 1 tablespoon
- Smoked paprika – 1 tablespoon
- Garlic powder – 1 tablespoon
- Onion powder – 1 tablespoon
- Mustard – 1 ½ teaspoon
- Cayenne pepper – ½ teaspoon

The Glaze

- Olive oil – 2 tablespoons
- Raspberry jam – ¾ cup
- Tabasco – 1 tablespoon

The Liquid

- Apple juice – 2 cups

The Heat

- Cherry wood chips, soak for an hour
- Apple wood chips, soak for an hour

Method

1. Pour water into a container then add salt, white sugar, and brown sugar to the water. Stir until dissolved.
2. Season the brine with rosemary sprigs, bay leaves, chopped onion, minced garlic, smoked paprika, and cayenne pepper then mix well.
3. Add the pork ribs to the brine and soak for overnight. Store in the fridge to keep it fresh.
4. On the next day, remove the pork ribs from the fridge and take the pork out of the brine.
5. Wash and rinse the pork ribs then pat it dry. Set aside.
6. Next, pour apple juice into an iron pan then place in the gas smoker.
7. Add the soaked wood chips to the tray and set it in the gas smoker.
8. Ignite your gas smoker and get it ready. Let it reach 225°F (107°C).
9. While waiting for the gas smoker, combine the rub ingredients—brown sugar, salt, black pepper, smoked paprika, garlic powder, onion powder, mustard, and cayenne pepper in a bowl then stir until well mixed.
10. Rub the pork ribs with the spice mixture and once the gas smoker is ready, place in the smoker.
11. Smoke the seasoned pork ribs for approximately 5 hours or until the internal temperature of the smoked pork has reached 185°F (85°C).
12. In the meantime, mix raspberry jam with olive oil and Tabasco then stir until incorporated.
13. Baste the raspberry sauce over the pork ribs and continue smoking for 30 minutes.
14. Remove the smoked pork from the smoker and transfer to a serving dish.
15. Serve and enjoy!

(Cooking Time 4 Hours 30 Minutes)
Ingredients for 10 servings
- Pork Loin (3-lb., 1.4-kg.)

The Marinade
- Garlic powder – 2 teaspoons
- Onion powder – 2 teaspoons
- Salt – 1 tablespoon
- Cola Coke – 1 cup
- Brown sugar – ½ cup
- Black pepper – 1 teaspoon
- Olive oil – ¼ cup

The Glaze
- Cherry preserves – ¾ cup
- Maple syrup – 3 tablespoons
- Worcestershire sauce – 1 tablespoon
- White vinegar – 2 tablespoons

The Liquid
- Apple juice – 2 cups

The Heat
- Cherry wood chips, soak for an hour
- Red Gum wood chips, soak for an hour

Method
1. Pour Cola Coke and olive oil into a container then season with garlic powder, onion powder, salt, brown sugar, and black pepper. Stir well.
2. Rub the pork tenderloin with the marinade mixture then marinate for at least 8 hours. Store in the fridge to keep it fresh.
3. On the next day, remove the pork tenderloin from the fridge and thaw at room temperature.
4. Pour apple juice into an iron pan then place in the gas smoker.
5. Add the soaked wood chips to the tray and set it in the gas smoker.
6. Ignite your gas smoker and get it ready. Let it reach 225°F (107°C).

7.   Once the gas smoker is ready, place the seasoned pork loin in the smoker and smoke for 4 hours.

8.   In the meantime, combine cherry preserves with maple syrup, Worcestershire sauce, and white vinegar. Stir until incorporated.

9.   After 4 hours of smoking or the internal temperature of the smoked pork loin has reached 145°F (63°C).

10.   Baste a half of the glaze mixture over the smoked pork loin then wrap with aluminum foil.

11.   Return the wrapped pork loin to the gas smoker and smoke for 30 minutes.

12.   When the smoked pork loin is done, remove from the gas smoker and unwrap it.

13.   Transfer to a serving dish then quickly drizzle the remaining glaze over the smoked pork loin while it is still hot.

14.   Cut the smoked pork loin into thick slices then serve.

15.   Enjoy!

(Cooking Time 4 Hours 30 Minutes)

Ingredients for 10 servings

- Pork Loin (4-lbs., 1.8-kg.)

The Brine

- Water – 3 quarts
- Salt – ¼ cup
- Brown sugar – 1 cup
- Minced garlic – 2 tablespoons
- Cumin – 1 ½ teaspoons
- Ground coriander – 1 ½ teaspoons
- Dried thyme – 1 teaspoon

The Rub

- Brown sugar – ¾ cup
- Salt – 1 tablespoon
- Black pepper – 1 tablespoon
- Garlic powder – 1 tablespoon
- Onion powder – 2 tablespoons
- Chipotle powder – 1 teaspoon
- Cinnamon – 2 teaspoons

The Glaze

- Peach preserves – 1 cup
- Corn oil – 2 tablespoons

The Liquid

- Apple juice – 2 cups

The Heat

- Cherry wood chips, soak for an hour
- Apple wood chips, soak for an hour

Method

1. Pour water into a container then season with salt and brown sugar. Stir until dissolved.
2. Add minced garlic, cumin, ground coriander, and dried thyme to the brine then put the pork loin into it. Soak for overnight and store in the fridge to keep it fresh.

3.   On the next day, remove the pork loin from the refrigerator and take it out from the brine.

4.   Wash and rinse the pork loin then pat it dry. Set aside.

5.   Combine the rub ingredients—brown sugar, salt, black pepper, garlic powder, onion powder, chipotle powder, and cinnamon in a bowl then mix well.

6.   Apply the rub mixture over the pork loin then let it sit for about 30 minutes.

7.   Next, pour apple juice into an iron pan then place in the gas smoker.

8.   Add the soaked wood chips to the tray and set it in the gas smoker.

9.   Ignite your gas smoker and get it ready. Let it reach 250°F (121°C).

10.   When the gas smoker is ready, place the seasoned pork loin in the smoker and smoke until the internal temperature of the smoked pork loin has reached 135°F (57°C). It will take approximately 4 hours.

11.   Once the internal temperature of the smoked pork loin hits 135°F (57°C), mix peach preserves with corn oil and baste over the smoked pork loin.

12.   Continue smoking until the internal temperature of the smoked pork loin has reached 145°F (63°C) and remove it from the smoker.

13.   Cut the juicy smoked pork loin into slices then serve.

14.   Enjoy.

(Cooking Time 6 Hours 30 Minutes)
Ingredients for 10 servings
- Pork Roast (6-lb., 2.7-kg.)

The Injection
- Fresh orange juice – ¾ cup
- Brown sugar – ¼ cup
- Salt – ½ teaspoon
- Worcestershire sauce – 1 tablespoon

The Rub
- Brown sugar – 3 tablespoons
- Grated orange zest – 2 teaspoons
- Garlic powder – 1 tablespoon
- Salt – 1 ½ tablespoons
- Smoked paprika – ½ tablespoon
- Chili powder – ¼ teaspoon
- Cumin – 1 teaspoon
- Cinnamon – 1 ½ teaspoons
- Ground clove – a pinch

The Glaze
- Orange juice – ¾ cup
- Apple cider vinegar – 3 tablespoons
- Cayenne pepper – 1 teaspoon
- Cinnamon – 1 teaspoon

The Liquid
- Water – 2 cups
- Lemon juice – 2 tablespoons

The Heat
- Cherry wood chips, soak for an hour
- Red Gum wood chips, soak for an hour

Method

1. Combine the entire injection ingredients—fresh orange juice, brown sugar, salt, and Worcestershire sauce then stir until dissolved. Fill into an injector.
2. Inject the pork roast with the mixture at several places then set aside.
3. Next, mix the grated orange zest with brown sugar, garlic powder, salt, smoked paprika, chili powder, cumin, cinnamon, and ground clove then apply over the pork roast. Set aside.
4. Pour apple juice into an iron pan then add lemon juice into the pan. Stir well and place in the gas smoker.
5. Add the soaked wood chips to the tray and set it in the gas smoker.
6. Ignite your gas smoker and get it ready. Let it reach 225°F (107°C).
7. Place the seasoned pork roast in the gas smoker and smoke for approximately 4 hours.
8. In the meantime, combine the glaze mixture—orange juice, apple cider vinegar, cayenne pepper, and cinnamon in a bowl then stir until incorporated.
9. After 4 hours of smoking, baste the glaze mixture over the pork roast and continues smoking for another 2 hours or until the internal temperature of smoked pork roast has reached 160°F (71°C).
10. Once it is done, remove the smoked pork roast from the gas smoker and transfer to a serving dish.
11. Quickly baste the remaining glaze mixture over the smoked pork roast then cut into slices.
12. Serve and enjoy.

(Cooking Time 8 Hours 30 Minutes)
Ingredients for 10 servings
- Pork butt (5-lb., 2.3-kg.)

The Marinade
- Beer – 3 cups
- Apple cider vinegar – ½ cup
- Black peppercorns – 1 ½ tablespoons

The Rub
- Brown sugar – 1 ½ cups
- Salt – 1 tablespoon
- Smoked paprika – 2 tablespoons
- Garlic powder – 2 tablespoons
- Onion powder – 3 tablespoons
- Black pepper – 1 tablespoon
- Cayenne powder – 1 tablespoon
- Chili powder – 1 ½ tablespoons
- Cumin – 2 teaspoons
- Apple cider vinegar – 3 tablespoons

The Sauce
- Butter – 2 tablespoons
- Diced onion- ¼ cup
- Minced garlic – 1 tablespoon
- Beer – ½ cup
- Brown sugar – ¾ cup
- Ketchup – ½ cup
- Tomato paste – ¼ cup
- Mustard – 2 tablespoons
- Liquid smoke – 1 tablespoon
- Cayenne pepper – 1 teaspoon
- Cumin – ½ teaspoon
- Salt – ½ teaspoon

- Black pepper – 1 teaspoon

The Liquid
- Beer – 1 cup
- Apple juice – 1 cup

The Heat
- Apple wood chips, soak for an hour

Method
1. Pour beer into a container then add apple cider vinegar and black peppercorns to the beer. Stir well.
2. Put the pork into the beer mixture then marinate for at least 4 hours.
3. In the meantime, combine the rub ingredients—brown sugar, salt, smoked paprika, garlic powder, onion powder, smoked paprika, cayenne powder, chili powder, cumin, and apple cider vinegar then mix well.
4. After 4 hours, take the pork butt out of the beer mixture then rub with the spice mixture. Let it sit for a few minutes.
5. Pour beer and apple juice into an iron pan then stir well. Place in the gas smoker.
6. Add the soaked wood chips to the tray and set it in the gas smoker.
7. Ignite your gas smoker and get it ready. Let it reach 225°F (107°C).
8. Place the seasoned pork butt in the gas smoker then smoke for 8 hours or until the internal temperature of the smoked pork but has reached 185°F (85°C).
9. Once it is done, take the smoked pork butt out of the gas smoker then let it cool for several minutes.
10. Using a fork or a sharp knife shred the smoked pork then place on a serving dish. Set aside.
11. Preheat a saucepan over medium heat then place butter in it.
12. When the butter is melted, stir in minced garlic and diced onion then sauté until wilted and aromatic. Remove from heat.
13. Add brown sugar, ketchup, tomato paste, mustard, liquid smoke, cayenne pepper, cumin, salt, and black pepper to the saucepan then pour beer into it. Stir well.
14. Drizzle the BBQ sauce over the smoked pulled pork then stir until combined.
15. Serve and enjoy.

CHAPTER-3 LAMB

Orange Marmalade Smoked Lamb Shank with Rosemary Marinade

(Cooking Time 6 Hours 10 Minutes)

Ingredients for 10 servings

- Lamb shanks (5-lb., 2.3-kg.)

The Marinade

- Olive oil – 1 cup
- Dried rosemary – 3 tablespoons
- Grated orange zest – 2 teaspoons
- Black pepper – 3 tablespoons
- Salt – 2 tablespoons
- Garlic powder – 2 teaspoons

The Glaze

- Orange marmalade - 1 cup
- Olive oil – ½ cup

The Liquid

- Water – 2 cups
- Lemon juice – 2 tablespoons

The Heat

- Hickory wood chips, soak for an hour

Method

1. Pour olive oil into a bowl then season with dried rosemary, grated orange zest, black pepper, salt, and garlic powder. Stir well.
2. Rub the lamb shank with the spice mixture then marinate for at least 8 hours.
3. Place the lamb shank in a container with a lid and store in the fridge to keep it fresh.
4. After 8 hours, remove the marinated lamb shank from the fridge and thaw at room temperature.
5. Pour water into an iron pan then add lemon juice to the water. Stir well and place in the gas smoker.
6. Add the soaked wood chips to the tray and set it in the gas smoker.
7. Ignite your gas smoker and get it ready. Let it reach 225°F (107°C).
8. Combine the orange marmalade with olive oil then stir well.

9. Baste the orange marmalade mixture over the lamb shank then wrap with aluminum foil.

10. Prick the wrapped lamb shank at several places and once the gas smoker is ready, place it in the smoker.

11. Smoke the lamb shank for 5 to 6 minutes or until the internal temperature of the lamb shank has reached 190°F (88°C).

12. Once it is done, remove the smoked lamb shank from the gas smoker and let it rest for a few minutes.

13. Unwrap the smoked lamb shank and transfer to a serving dish.

14. Serve and enjoy.

(Cooking Time 10 Hours 10 Minutes)

Ingredients for 10 servings
- Lamb shoulder (6-lb., 2.7-kg.)

The Injection
- Apple cider vinegar – 1 ½ cups

The Rub
- Salt – 1 ½ tablespoons
- Grated lemon zest – 1 tablespoon
- Black pepper – 2 tablespoons
- Mustard – 2 tablespoons
- Smoked paprika – 2 tablespoons
- Cumin – 1 ½ teaspoons
- Garlic powder – 2 tablespoons
- Brown sugar – ¼ cup
- Cayenne pepper – 2 teaspoons

The Spray
- Apple juice – 1 ½ cups
- Apple cider vinegar – ¾ cup

The Liquid
- Apple juice – 3 cups

The Heat
- Hickory wood chips, soak for an hour
- Apple wood chips, soak for an hour

Method
1. Inject the lamb shoulder with apple cider vinegar at several places then set aside.
2. Combine the rub ingredients—salt, grated lemon zest, black pepper, mustard, smoked paprika, cumin, garlic powder, brown sugar, and cayenne pepper then apply over the lamb shoulder.
3. Pour apple juice into an iron pan then place in the gas smoker.
4. Add the soaked wood chips to the tray and set it in the gas smoker.
5. Ignite your gas smoker and get it ready. Let it reach 200°F (93°C).
6. Place the seasoned lamb shoulder in the gas smoker and smoke for 10 hours.

7.   Spray the apple juice and apple cider vinegar mixture once every 2 hours and occasionally check the internal temperature of the smoked lamb shoulder.

8.   Once the internal temperature of the smoked lamb shoulder has reached 190°F (88°C), remove it from the gas smoker.

9.   Using a sharp knife or a fork shred the smoked lamb shoulder and place on a serving dish.

10.   Serve and enjoy.

Wine Marinade Smoked Lamb Ribs with Sticky Honey Glaze

(Cooking Time 5 Hours 10 Minutes)

Ingredients for 10 servings

- Lamb ribs (5.5-lb., 2.5-kg.)

The Marinade

- Dry white wine – 2 cups
- Soy sauce – ½ cup
- Lemon juice – ½ cup
- Honey – 3 tablespoons
- Olive oil – 2 tablespoons
- Garlic powder – 2 teaspoons
- Onion powder – 2 teaspoons
- Salt – 1 ¼ tablespoons
- Black pepper – 2 teaspoons
- Cinnamon – 2 teaspoons

The Glaze

- Honey – 1 ½ cups
- Soy sauce – ½ cup
- Dijon mustard – 3 tablespoons

The Liquid

- Water – 2 cups
- Ground ginger – 1 teaspoon

The Heat

- Apple wood chips, soak for an hour
- Red Gum wood chips, soak for an hour

Method

1.   Combine the marinade ingredients—dry white wine, soy sauce, lemon juice, honey, olive oil, garlic powder, onion powder, salt, black pepper, and cinnamon. Mix well.

2.   Season the lamb ribs with the spice mixture then marinate for overnight.

3.   Place the seasoned lamb ribs in a container with a lid and store in the fridge to keep it fresh.

4.   On the next day, remove the seasoned lamb ribs from the fridge and thaw at room temperature.

5.   Pour water into an iron pan then add ginger to the water. Stir until dissolved and place in the gas smoker.

6.   Add the soaked wood chips to the tray and set it in the gas smoker.

7.   Ignite your gas smoker and get it ready. Let it reach 225°F (107°C).

8.   Place the seasoned lamb ribs in the smoker and smoke for approximately 5 hours or until the internal temperature of the smoked lamb ribs has reached 165°F (74°C).

9.   In the meantime, mix honey with soy sauce and Dijon mustard. Stir until incorporated.

10.   Once the smoked lamb ribs have reached the desired temperature, remove from the gas smoker and quickly glaze with the honey mixture.

11.   Place the glazed smoked lamb ribs on a serving dish then serve.

12.   Enjoy!

Smoked Lamb Leg with Fresh Herbs Marinade and Rub

(Cooking Time 5 Hours 10 Minutes)

Ingredients for 10 servings

- Lamb leg (4-lbs., 1.8-kg.)

The Marinade

- Lemon juice – ¼ cup
- Grated lemon zest – 2 teaspoons
- Olive oil – ½ cup
- Minced garlic – 3 tablespoons
- Fresh oregano – ¼ cup
- Fresh thyme – 2 teaspoons
- Diced onion – ½ cup
- Freshly ground black pepper – 2 teaspoons

The Rub

- Olive oil – 2 tablespoons
- Salt – 1 tablespoon
- Fresh sage leaves – 10
- Freshly chopped rosemary leaves – 3 tablespoons
- Fresh thyme leaves – 2 tablespoons
- Red chili flakes – 2 teaspoons
- Fennel seeds – 1 teaspoons
- Freshly ground black pepper – ½ teaspoon

The Liquid

- Water – 2 cups

The Heat

- Hickory wood chips, soak for an hour

Method

1. Start by combining olive oil with lemon juice then add grated lemon zest, minced garlic, diced onion, oregano, thyme, and black pepper. Stir well.
2. Apply the spice mixture over the lamb leg then marinate for at least 4 hours.
3. In the meantime, combine sage leaves with rosemary, thyme, red chili flakes, fennel seeds, salt, and black pepper then mix well.
4. Drizzle olive oil into the fresh herbs mixture then mix until combined.

5.   After 4 hours of the marinade, rub the lamb leg with the fresh herbs mixture. Set aside.
6.   Pour water into an iron pan and place in the gas smoker.
7.   Add the soaked wood chips to the tray and set it in the gas smoker.
8.   Ignite your gas smoker and get it ready. Let it reach 225°F (107°C).
9.   When the gas smoker is ready, place the seasoned lamb leg in the smoker and smoke for approximately 5 hours.
10.   Wait until the internal temperature of the smoked lamb leg has reached 145°F (63°C), remove from the smoker and transfer to a serving dish.
11.   Serve and enjoy.

(Cooking Time 5 Hours 10 Minutes)

Ingredients for 10 servings

- Lamb chop (4-lbs., 1.8-kg.)

The Rub

- Ground coffee – 2 tablespoons
- Salt – 1 tablespoon
- Smoked paprika – 2 tablespoons
- Chili powder – 1 tablespoon
- Brown sugar – 3 tablespoons
- Oregano – 2 teaspoons
- Garlic powder – 2 teaspoons
- Onion powder – 2 teaspoons
- Black pepper – 1 teaspoon
- Cocoa powder – 1 teaspoon
- Coriander – 1 teaspoon

The Glaze

- Brewed coffee – ½ cup
- Molasses – 3 tablespoons
- Apple cider vinegar – 3 tablespoons
- Rum – 1 tablespoon
- Garlic powder – 2 teaspoons
- Cinnamon – ½ teaspoon
- Allspice – ¼ teaspoon
- Red chili flakes – 2 teaspoons

The Liquid

- Water – 2 cups

The Heat

- Mesquite wood chips, soak for an hour

Method

1. Place ground coffee, salt, smoked paprika, chili powder; brown sugar, oregano, garlic powder, onion powder, black pepper, cocoa powder, and coriander in a bowl then mix well.

2.   Rub the lamb chop with the spice mixture then set a side.

3.   Pour water into an iron pan and place in the gas smoker.

4.   Add the soaked wood chips to the tray and set it in the gas smoker.

5.   Ignite your gas smoker and get it ready. Let it reach 225°F (107°C).

6.   Place the seasoned lamb chop in the gas smoker and smoke for 5 hours or until the internal temperature of the smoked lamb chop has reached 190°F (88°C).

7.   30 minutes before the smoking time ends, combine brewed coffee with molasses, apple cider vinegar, garlic powder, cinnamon, allspice, and red chili flakes. Mix well.

8.   Pour rum into the coffee glaze mixture then stir until incorporated.

9.   Once the smoked lamb chop is done, take it out of the gas smoker and quickly baste the glaze mixture over the smoked lamb chops.

10.   Wrap the glazed smoked lamb with aluminum foil then let it rest for approximately an hour.

11.   Unwrap the aluminum foil then serve.

12.   Enjoy.

CHAPTER-4 POULTRY

Sweet Brown Smoked Chicken Chili Oregano

(Cooking Time 3 Hours 10 Minutes)

Ingredients for 10 servings

- A whole chicken (4.5-lb., 2-kg.)

The Brine

- Water – 2 quarts
- Salt – 2 tablespoons
- Brown sugar – ¼ cup
- Lemon juice – 2 tablespoons

The Marinade

- Brown sugar – ½ cup
- Chili powder – 2 ½ tablespoons
- Smoked paprika – 1 ½ tablespoons
- Onion powder – 1 tablespoon
- Garlic powder – 1 tablespoon
- Oregano – 1 ½ tablespoons
- Salt – 1 ½ teaspoons

The Liquid

- Apple juice – 2 cups

The Heat

- Hickory wood chips, soak for an hour
- Apple wood chips, soak for an hour

Method

1. Add salt and brown sugar to a container then pour water into it.
2. Drizzle lemon juice over the water and stir until dissolved.
3. Next, score the chicken at several places then soak into the brine mixture for at least 8 hours. Store in the fridge to keep it fresh.
4. After 8 hours, remove the chicken from the brine then wash and rinse it. Pat the chicken dry.
5. Combine the marinade ingredients—brown sugar, chili powder, smoked paprika, onion powder, garlic powder, oregano, and salt in a bowl then mix well.

6. Rub the spice mixture over the chicken then marinate for at least an hour.
7. In the meantime, pour apple juice into an iron pan then place in the gas smoker.
8. Add the soaked wood chips to the tray and set it in the gas smoker.
9. Ignite your gas smoker and get it ready. Let it reach 275°F (135°C).
10. Once it is ready, place the seasoned chicken in the gas smoker and smoke for 2 to 3 hours or until the internal temperature of the smoked chicken has reached 170°F (77°C).
11. Remove the smoked chicken from the gas smoker and transfer to a serving dish.
12. Serve and enjoy.

(Cooking Time 1 Hour 30 Minutes)

Ingredients for 10 servings

- Chicken wings (3-lb., 1.4-kg.)

The Brine

- Cold water – 2 quarts
- Salt – ½ cup
- White sugar – ½ cup
- White vinegar (1/4 cup)
- Chili powder – 2 teaspoons
- Black pepper – 2 tablespoons
- White pepper – 1 tablespoons

The Rub

- Vegetable oil – ½ cup
- Brown sugar – ¾ cup
- Smoked paprika – 3 tablespoons
- Chili powder – 2 tablespoons
- Onion powder – 1 tablespoon
- Garlic powder – 1 tablespoon
- Cumin – 1 teaspoon
- Salt – ½ tablespoon
- Dried rosemary – 1 teaspoon

The Glaze

- Butter – ½ cup
- Tabasco – 3 tablespoons
- Honey – ½ cup
- Garlic powder – 1 teaspoon

The Liquid

- Apple juice – 2 cups

The Heat

- Cherry wood chips, soak for an hour
- Apple wood chips, soak for an hour

Method

1. Pour cold water into a container then season with salt, white sugar, white vinegar, chili powder, black pepper, and white pepper. Stir until dissolved.
2. Add the chicken wings to the brine mixture and soak for at least 4 hours.
3. After 4 hours, take the chicken wings out of the brine then wash and rinse them. Pat the chicken wings dry.
4. Combine brown sugar, smoked paprika, chili powder, onion powder, garlic powder, cumin, salt, and dried rosemary then stir well.
5. Pour vegetable oil over the dry mixture then mix until combined.
6. Rub the chicken wings with the spice mixture then set aside.
7. Next, pour apple juice into an iron pan then place in the gas smoker.
8. Add the soaked wood chips to the tray and set it in the gas smoker.
9. Ignite your gas smoker and get it ready. Let it reach 275°F (135°C).
10. Arrange the seasoned chicken wings in the gas smoker and smoke for approximately an hour and 30 minutes or until the internal temperature of the smoked chicken wings has reached 170°F (77°C).
11. In the meantime, preheat a saucepan over low heat then place butter in it.
12. Once the butter is melted, remove from heat then add Tabasco and garlic. Stir well and let it cool for a few minutes.
13. Pour honey into the melted butter then stir until incorporated.
14. Once the smoked chicken wings are done, remove from the gas smoker and transfer to a serving dish.
15. Quickly baste the smoked chicken wings with the butter and honey mixture then serve.
16. Enjoy!

(Cooking Time 2 Hours)
Ingredients for 10 servings
- Chicken drumsticks (4-lbs., 1.8-kg.)

The Marinade
- Sesame oil – ¾ cup
- Lemon juice – ¼ cup
- Grated lemon zest – 1 teaspoon
- Worcestershire sauce – ¼ cup
- Beer – ¾ cup
- Salt – 1 tablespoon
- Black pepper – 1 teaspoon

The Glaze
- Sesame oil – ¼ cup
- Ketchup – 1 cup
- Beer – ½ cup
- Lemon juice – 2 tablespoons
- Honey – ¼ cup
- Soy sauce – 2 tablespoons
- Grated lemon zest – 1 teaspoon
- Minced garlic – 2 tablespoons
- Ground ginger – ½ teaspoon
- Mustard – 2 tablespoons

The Liquid
- Beer – 2 cups

The Heat
- Hickory wood chips, soak for an hour
- Apple wood chips, soak for an hour

Method
1. Marinate the chicken drumsticks with the marinade mixture—sesame oil, lemon juice, grated lemon zest, Worcestershire sauce, beer, salt, and black pepper, for 4 hours.

2.	Place the marinated chicken drumsticks in a container with a lid and store in the fridge to keep the chicken drumsticks fresh.

3.	After 4 hours, remove the marinated chicken drumsticks from the fridge and thaw at room temperature.

4.	Next, pour beer into an iron pan then place in the gas smoker.

5.	Add the soaked wood chips to the tray and set it in the gas smoker.

6.	Ignite your gas smoker and get it ready. Let it reach 275°F (135°C).

7.	Arrange the seasoned chicken drumsticks in the gas smoker and smoke for an hour.

8.	In the meantime, pour sesame oil, ketchup, beer, lemon juice, honey, and soy sauce into a bowl then stir until incorporated.

9.	Season with grated lemon zest, minced garlic, ground ginger, and mustard. Mix well.

10.	After an hour of smoking, baste the chicken drumsticks with the glaze mixture and repeat once every 20 minutes.

11.	Continue smoking until the internal temperature of the smoked chicken drumsticks has reached 170°F (77°C).

12.	Once the smoked chicken drumsticks are done, remove from the gas smoker and arrange on a serving dish.

13.	Serve and enjoy.

(Cooking Time 2 Hours)
Ingredients for 10 servings
- Chicken thighs (5-lb., 2.3-kg.)

The Rub
- Brown sugar – 1 ½ cups
- Salt – 1 ¼ tablespoons
- Garlic powder – 2 tablespoons
- Onion powder – 2 tablespoons
- Smoked paprika – 2 teaspoons
- Black pepper – 1 teaspoon
- Coriander – 2 teaspoons
- Dijon mustard – 2 tablespoons
- Honey – 3 tablespoons

The Sauce
- Maple syrup – ¾ cup
- Bourbon – ½ cup
- Ketchup – ¾ cup
- Vegetable oil – 3 tablespoons
- Cider vinegar – 2 tablespoons
- Dijon mustard – 1 tablespoon
- Garlic powder – 1 teaspoon
- Black pepper – ½ teaspoon

The Liquid
- Apple juice – 2 cups

The Heat
- Mesquite wood chips, soak for an hour
- Apple wood chips, soak for an hour

Method
1. Place the rub ingredients—brown sugar, salt, garlic powder, onion powder, smoked paprika, black pepper, and ground coriander in a bowl. Mix well.
2. Add Dijon mustard and honey to the rub mixture then stir until combined.

3.   Rub the chicken thighs with the spice mixture then set aside.

4.   Next, pour apple juice into an iron pan then place in the gas smoker.

5.   Add the soaked wood chips to the tray and set it in the gas smoker.

6.   Ignite your gas smoker and get it ready. Let it reach 275°F (135°C).

7.   When the gas smoker is ready, place the seasoned chicken thighs in the gas smoker and smoke for approximately 2 hours.

8.   In the meantime, pour maple syrup into a saucepan then add the remaining sauce ingredients—bourbon, ketchup, vegetable oil, cider vinegar, Dijon mustard, garlic powder, and black pepper. Stir well and bring to a simmer.

9.   Remove the sauce from heat and let it cool.

10.   Once the internal temperature of the smoked chicken thighs has reached 170°F (77°C), remove from the gas smoker and transfer to a serving dish.

11.   Quickly baste the sauce over the smoked chicken thighs and serve.

12.   Enjoy!

(Cooking Time 2 Hours)

Ingredients for 10 servings

- Chicken breast (4-lbs., 1.8-kg.)

The Rub

- Brown sugar – ¼ cup
- Salt – 1 tablespoon
- Ground coffee – 2 tablespoons
- Garlic powder – 2 teaspoons
- Onion powder – 1 teaspoon
- Cumin – ½ teaspoon
- Cayenne pepper – ½ teaspoon
- Black pepper – 1 teaspoon

The Sauce

- Butter – 3 tablespoons
- Brewed coffee – ¾ cup
- Balsamic vinegar – 2 tablespoons
- Ketchup – 3 tablespoons
- Onion powder – 1 teaspoon
- Red chili powder – 1 teaspoon
- Brown sugar – 3 tablespoons
- Black pepper – ½ teaspoon

The Liquid

- Water – 2 cups

The Heat

- Hickory wood chips, soak for an hour

Method

1. Combine brown sugar with salt, ground coffee, garlic powder, onion powder, cumin, cayenne pepper, and black pepper then mix well.
2. Rub the chicken breast with the spice mixture then set aside.
3. Next, pour water into an iron pan then place in the gas smoker.
4. Add the soaked wood chips to the tray and set it in the gas smoker.

5.   Ignite your gas smoker and get it ready. Let it reach 275°F (135°C).

6.   Place the seasoned chicken breast in the gas smoker then smoke for approximately 2 hours.

7.   Wait until the internal temperature of the smoked chicken breast has reached 170°F (77°C) and remove from the gas smoker. Transfer to a serving dish.

8.   Quickly melt butter in a saucepan then add brewed coffee to the saucepan.

9.   Remove the melted butter from heat then add balsamic vinegar and ketchup.

10.   Season the sauce with onion powder, red chili powder, brown sugar, and black pepper then stir until incorporated.

11.   Drizzle the sauce over the smoked chicken breast then serve.

12.   Enjoy.

CHAPTER-5 FISH

Aromatic Orange Low Smoked Trout

(Cooking Time 4 Hours 10 Minutes)
Ingredients for 10 servings
- Whole trout (3-lb., 1.4-kg.)

The Marinade
- Orange juice – 4 cups
- White sugar – ¼ cup
- Brown sugar – ¼ cup
- Salt – 2 tablespoons
- Chili powder – 1 tablespoon
- Cayenne pepper – 1 tablespoon
- Garlic powder – 1 tablespoon
- Onion powder – 1 tablespoon
- Cinnamon – ½ teaspoon

The Glaze
- Butter – ¼ cup

The Liquid
- Water – 2 cups
- Sliced oranges – ½ cup

The Heat
- Alder wood chips, soak for an hour

Method
1.   Pour orange juice into a container then add white sugar, brown sugar, salt, chili powder, cayenne pepper, garlic powder, onion powder, and cinnamon. Stir until dissolved.
2.   Put the trout into the container and make sure that the trout is completely soaked.
3.   Marinate for overnight and store in the fridge to keep it fresh.
4.   On the next day, remove the trout from the fridge and take it out of the marinade. Thaw at room temperature.
5.   Pour water into an iron pan then add sliced orange in the pan. Place in the gas smoker.
6.   Add the soaked wood chips to the tray and set it in the gas smoker.
7.   Ignite your gas smoker and get it ready. Let it reach 200°F (93°C).
8.   Place the seasoned trout in the gas smoker then smoke for approximately 3 to 4 hours. Baste butter over the trout once every 30 minutes.
9.   Once the internal temperature of the smoked trout has reached 145°F (63°C), remove from the gas smoker and transfer to a serving dish.
10.   Serve and enjoy.

(Cooking Time 4 Hours 10 Minutes)

Ingredients for 10 servings

- Salmon fillet (3-lb., 1.4-kg.)

The Brine

- Brown sugar – ½ cup
- Salt – ½ tablespoon
- Soy sauce – 2 cups
- Dry white wine – 1 cup
- Onion powder – 1 teaspoon
- Garlic powder – 1 teaspoon
- Black pepper – ½ teaspoon
- Tabasco – 1 teaspoon
- Water – 2 cups

The Liquid

- Water – 2 cups
- Ground ginger – 1 teaspoon

The Heat

- Alder wood chips, soak for an hour

Method

1. Combine brown sugar with salt, garlic powder, onion powder, and black pepper. Mix well.
2. Pour water over the dry mixture then add Tabasco, dry white wine, and soy sauce. Stir until incorporated.
3. Put the salmon fillet into the brine mixture and soak for 8 hours.
4. Remove the salmon from the brine then wash and rinse it. Pat it dry.
5. Pour water into an iron pan then add ginger to the pan. Place in the gas smoker.
6. Add the soaked wood chips to the tray and set it in the gas smoker.
7. Ignite your gas smoker and get it ready. Let it reach 200°F (93°C).
8. Place the salmon in the gas smoker and smoke for 2 hours.
9. Increase the temperature of the gas smoker to 275°F (135°C) and continue smoking the salmon until the internal temperature has reached 165°F (74°C).
10. Remove from the gas smoker and transfer to a serving dish.
11. Serve and enjoy.

(Cooking Time 3 Hours 10 Minutes)

Ingredients for 10 servings

- Tuna fillet (3-lb., 1.4-kg.)

The Rub

- Lemon juice – ¼ cup
- Olive oil – 2 tablespoons
- Salt – ½ tablespoon
- Brown sugar – ¼ cup
- Garlic powder – 1 teaspoon

The Liquid

- Water – 2 cups
- Ground ginger – ½ teaspoon
- Lemon juice – 1 tablespoon

The Heat

- Alder wood chips, soak for an hour
- Peach wood chips, soak for an hour

Method

1. Pour lemon juice and olive oil into a bowl then season with garlic powder, brown sugar, and salt. Stir until combined.
2. Rub the tuna fillet with the spice mixture then marinate for 2 hours.
3. Pour water into an iron pan then add ginger and lemon juice to the pan. Place in the gas smoker.
4. Add the soaked wood chips to the tray and set it in the gas smoker.
5. Ignite your gas smoker and get it ready. Let it reach 200°F (93°C).
6. Place the seasoned tuna in the gas smoker and smoke for approximately 3 hours.
7. Wait until the internal temperature has reached 145°F (63°C) and remove the smoked tuna from the gas smoker.
8. Transfer the smoked tuna to a serving dish then serve.
9. Enjoy.

(Cooking Time 3 Hours 10 Minutes)
Ingredients for 10 servings
- Snapper fillet (3-lb., 1.4-kg.)

The Brine
- Tea leaves – 3 tablespoons
- Water – 4 cups
- Salt – 1 tablespoon
- Brown sugar – ½ cup
- Black pepper – 1 teaspoon
- Garlic powder – 1 tablespoon
- Sliced lemon – ½ cup

The Rub
- Cumin – 2 teaspoons
- Coriander – 1 teaspoon
- Fennel seeds – 2 teaspoons
- Salt – ½ tablespoon
- Brown sugar – 3 tablespoons

The Liquid
- Brewed tea – 2 cups
- Lemon juice – 2 tablespoons

The Heat
- Alder wood chips, soak for an hour
- Peach wood chips, soak for an hour

Method
1. Place tealeaves, salt, brown sugar, black pepper, and garlic powder in a container then stir well.
2. Add sliced lemon to the brine mixture then put the snapper fillet into the container.
3. Soak the snapper for overnight and store it in the fridge to keep it fresh.
4. On the next day, take the snapper out of the brine then wash and rinse it. Pat it dry.
5. Next, combine the rub ingredients—cumin, coriander, fennel seeds, salt, and brown sugar. Mix well.

6.   Rub the snapper with the spice mixture then let it rest for a few minutes.

7.   Pour brewed tea into the iron pan then add lemon juice to the pan. Place in the gas smoker.

8.   Add the soaked wood chips to the tray and set it in the gas smoker.

9.   Ignite your gas smoker and get it ready. Let it reach 200°F (93°C).

10.   Place the snapper in the gas smoker and smoke for approximately 3 hours or until the internal temperature has reached 145°F (63°C).

11.   Once it is done, remove from the gas smoker and transfer the smoked snapper to a serving dish.

12.   Serve and enjoy.

CHAPTER-6 SEAFOOD

Brandy Smoked Oyster

(Cooking Time 2 Hours 10 Minutes)

Ingredients for 10 servings

- Oysters without shells (2-lbs., 0.9-kg.)

The Marinade

- Water – 1 ½ quarts
- Soy sauce – 2 tablespoons
- Hot sauce – 1 teaspoon
- Salt – ¼ cup
- Garlic powder – 1 tablespoon
- Onion powder – 1 tablespoon
- Black pepper – ½ teaspoon
- Brown sugar – ½ cup
- Brandy – ½ cup

The Glaze

- Olive oil – 3 tablespoons

The Liquid

- Water – 2 cups

The Heat

- Alder wood chips, soak for an hour

Method

1. Place salt, brown sugar, garlic powder, onion powder, and black pepper in a container then mix well.
2. Pour water together with soy sauce, hot sauce, and brandy over the dry mixture then stir until combined.
3. Add oysters to the container then rub with the spice mixture.
4. Marinate the oysters for overnight and store in the fridge to keep it fresh.
5. On the next day, remove the marinated oysters from the fridge and thaw at room temperature.

6.   Pour water into an iron pan then place in the gas smoker.

7.   Add the soaked wood chips to the tray and set it in the gas smoker.

8.   Ignite your gas smoker and get it ready. Let it reach 225°F (107°C).

9.   Place the marinated oysters in an aluminum pan then place in the gas smoker.

10.   Smoke the oysters for approximately 2 hours or until tender then remove from the gas smoker.

11.   Quickly drizzle olive oil over the smoked oysters then stir to coat.

12.   Serve and enjoy.

(Cooking Time 20 Minutes)
Ingredients for 10 servings
- Fresh shrimps (3-lb., 1.4-kg.)

The Rub
- Olive oil – ¼ cup
- Salt – ½ tablespoon
- Black pepper – 1 teaspoon

The Glaze
- Butter – ¼ cup
- Minced garlic – 1 tablespoon

The Liquid
- Water – 2 cups

The Heat
- Alder wood chips, soak for an hour

Method
1. Pour water into an iron pan then place in the gas smoker.
2. Add the soaked wood chips to the tray and set it in the gas smoker.
3. Ignite your gas smoker and get it ready. Let it reach 225°F (107°C).
4. Add salt and black pepper to the olive oil then mix well.
5. Rub the shrimps with the spice mixture then arrange in the gas smoker.
6. Smoke the shrimps for approximately 20 minutes or until the smoked shrimps are cooked through.
7. Once it is done, remove from the gas smoker and transfer to a serving dish.
8. Serve and enjoy.

(Cooking Time 30 Minutes)
Ingredients for 10 servings
- Crab (5-lb., 2.3-kg.)

The Glaze
- Butter – 1 cup
- Minced garlic – 3 tablespoons
- Black pepper – 1 tablespoon

The Sauce
- Champagne Vinegar – ¾ cup
- Diced onion – 2 tablespoons
- Black pepper – ½ teaspoon

The Liquid
- Water – 2 cups

The Heat
- Pecan wood chips, soak for an hour

Method
1. Add diced onion and black pepper to champagne vinegar then stir well.
2. Let the sauce rests for several hours before serving and store in the fridge to keep it fresh.
3. Pour water into the iron pan then place in the gas smoker.
4. Spread the soaked wood chips in the tray and set in the gas smoker.
5. Ignite your gas smoker and get it ready. Let it reach 250°F (121°C).
6. Place the crabs in the gas smoker then smoke for 15 minutes.
7. In the meantime, melt butter over low heat then stir in minced garlic to the saucepan. Sauté until aromatic and lightly golden brown.
8. Remove from heat and add black pepper to the melted butter. Stir well.
9. After 15 minutes of smoking, baste the crabs with the melted butter then continue smoking for 15 minutes.
10. Once it is done, remove the smoked crabs from the gas smoker and transfer to a serving dish.
11. Drizzle the champagne vinegar sauce over the smoked crabs then serve.
12. Enjoy.

(Cooking Time 45 Minutes)
Ingredients for 10 servings
- Scallop (3-lb., 1.4-kg.)

The Spices
- Smoked paprika – 1 teaspoon
- Lemon juice – 3 tablespoons
- Canola oil – 3 tablespoons
- Salt – ½ tablespoon
- Cumin – 1 teaspoon
- Pepper – ¼ teaspoon

The Liquid
- Water – 2 cups
- Lemon juice – 2 tablespoons

The Heat
- Alder wood chips, soak for an hour

Method
1. Pour water into the iron pan then add lemon juice to the pan. Place in the gas smoker.
2. Spread the soaked wood chips in the tray and set in the gas smoker.
3. Ignite your gas smoker and get it ready. Let it reach 225°F (107°C).
4. Spread the scallop in an aluminum pan then alternately drizzle lemon juice and canola oil over the scallops.
5. Sprinkle the smoked paprika, salt, cumin, and peppers on top then carefully stir until the scallops are completely seasoned.
6. Place the scallops in the gas smoker and smoke for 45 minutes or until cooked through.
7. Once it is done, remove the scallops from the gas smoker and transfer to a serving dish.
8. Serve and enjoy.

CHAPTER-7 GAME

Smoked Venison Tenderloin with Rosemary

(Cooking Time 4 Hours 10 Minutes)

Ingredients for 10 servings

- Venison Tenderloin (6-lb., 2.7-kg.)

The Brine

- Water – 1 gallon
- Soy sauce – ¾ cup
- Salt – ¾ cup
- Brown sugar – ¾ cup
- Worcestershire sauce – ¼ cup
- Molasses – ½ cup
- Pepper – 2 tablespoons
- Dried rosemary – 1 tablespoon
- Bay leaves – 2

The Rub

- Chili powder – 2 tablespoon
- Salt – 1 ½ tablespoons
- Black pepper – 2 tablespoons
- Garlic powder – 2 tablespoons
- Onion powder – 2 tablespoons
- Brown sugar – ¾ cup
- Mustard – 2 tablespoons

The Liquid

- Water – 2 cups

The Heat

- Cherry wood chips, soak for an hour

Method

1. Pour water into a container then add soy sauce, salt, brown sugar, Worcestershire sauce, molasses, pepper, and dried rosemary. Stir until dissolved.
2. Add dried rosemary and bay leaves to the brine mixture then mix until combined.
3. Put the venison tenderloin into the brine mixture then soak for overnight.

4.   On the next day, take the venison tenderloin out of the brine then wash and rinse it. Pat it dry.

5.   Next, combine the rub ingredients—chili powder, salt, black pepper, garlic powder, onion powder, brown sugar, and mustard in a bowl then mix well.

6.   Rub the venison tenderloin with the spice mixture then set aside.

7.   Pour water into an iron pan then place in the gas smoker.

8.   Add the soaked wood chips to the tray and set it in the gas smoker.

9.   Ignite your gas smoker and get it ready. Let it reach 225°F (107°C).

10.   Place the seasoned venison tenderloin in the gas smoker and smoke for 2 hours.

11.   Increase the temperature of the gas smoker to 250°F (121°C) and continue smoking the venison tenderloin for another 2 hours.

12.   Once the internal temperature of the smoked venison tenderloin has reached 160°F (71°C), remove from the gas smoker and transfer to a serving dish.

13.   Serve and enjoy.

(Cooking Time 3 Hours 10 Minutes)
Ingredients for 10 servings
- Rabbit (3-lb., 1.4-kg.)

The Brine
- Water – 1 gallon
- Fresh basils – 3 cups
- Oregano – ¼ cup
- Sugar – ¼ cup
- Minced garlic – ½ cup
- Red wine vinegar – ½ cup

The Rub
- Smoked paprika – ½ cup
- Cayenne pepper – 2 tablespoons
- Chili powder – 2 tablespoons
- Garlic powder – ¼ cup
- Onion powder – ¼ cup
- Black pepper – 1 tablespoon
- Salt – ½ tablespoon
- Dried oregano – 1 tablespoons
- Dried thyme – 2 tablespoons
- Italian seasoning – 2 tablespoons

The Liquid
- Water – 2 cups

The Heat
- Mesquite wood chips, soak for an hour

Method
1. Combine the brine ingredients into a container then mix well.
2. Add the rabbit to the brine mixture then soak for at least 4 hours.
3. After 4 hours, remove the rabbit from the brine mixture then wash and rinse it. Pat it dry.

4.   Next, combine the rub ingredients—smoked paprika, cayenne powder, chili powder, garlic powder, onion powder, black pepper, salt, dried oregano, dried thyme, and Italian seasoning in a bowl then mix well.

5.   Rub the rabbit with the spice mixture then set aside.

6.   Pour water into an iron pan then place in the gas smoker.

7.   Add the soaked wood chips to the tray and set it in the gas smoker.

8.   Ignite your gas smoker and get it ready. Let it reach 250°F (121°C).

9.   Place the seasoned rabbit in the gas smoker and smoke until the internal temperature has reached 165°F (74°C). It usually takes approximately 3 hours.

10.   Once it is done, remove the smoked rabbit from the gas smoker and transfer to a serving dish.

11.   Serve and enjoy.

(Cooking Time 3 Hours 10 Minutes)

Ingredients for 10 servings

- Pigeons (4-lbs., 1.8-kg.)

The Brine

- Water – 1 gallon
- Brown sugar – 2 cups
- Salt – ½ cup
- Tea leaves – ¼ cup
- Lemon juice – 3 tablespoons

The Rub

- Dried tea leaves – 2 tablespoons
- Ground coffee – ¾ tablespoons
- Onion powder – 2 teaspoons
- Garlic powder – 2 tablespoons
- Salt – ½ tablespoon

The Liquid

- Brewed tea – 2 cups

The Heat

- Alder wood chips, soak for an hour
- Apple wood chips, soak for an hour

Method

1. Pour water into a container then add brown sugar, salt, lemon juice, and tea. Stir well.
2. Put the pigeons into the brine mixture then soak for 4 hours.
3. Take the pigeons out of the brine mixture then pat it dry.
4. Rub the pigeon with a mixture of dried tea, ground coffee, onion powder, garlic powder, and salt. Set aside.
5. Pour brewed coffee into an iron pan then place in the gas smoker.
6. Add the soaked wood chips to the tray and set it in the gas smoker.
7. Ignite your gas smoker and get it ready. Let it reach 275°F (135°C).
8. Place the seasoned pigeon in the gas smoker and smoke for 2 to 3 hours.
9. Wait until the internal temperature of the smoked pigeon has reached 170°F (77°C) and remove from the gas smoker.
10. Transfer the smoked pigeon to a serving dish then serve.
11. Enjoy!

CHAPTER-8 VEGETABLES

Smoked Portobello Mushrooms Chili

(Cooking Time 45 Minutes)

Ingredients for 10 servings

- Portobello mushrooms (2-lbs., 0.9-kg.)

The Spices

- Butter – 3 tablespoons
- Worcestershire sauce – 1 ½ tablespoons
- Salt – ¼ tablespoon
- Pepper – ½ teaspoon
- Dried rosemary – ½ teaspoon
- Oregano – ½ teaspoon

The Liquid

- Water – 2 cups

The Heat

- Apple wood chips, soak for an hour

Method

1. Place butter into a saucepan then melt over low heat.
2. Once the butter is melted, remove from heat then drizzle over the mushrooms.
3. Sprinkle salt, pepper, dried rosemary, and oregano over the mushrooms then add Worcestershire sauce. Toss to coat.
4. Next, pour water into an iron pan then place in the gas smoker.
5. Add the soaked wood chips to the tray and set it in the gas smoker.
6. Ignite your gas smoker and get it ready. Let it reach 225°F (107°C).
7. Place the mushrooms in the gas smoker and smoke for approximately 45 minutes.
8. Remove the smoked mushrooms from the gas smoker and transfer to a serving dish.
9. Serve and enjoy.

(Cooking Time 45 Minutes)
Ingredients for 10 servings
- Eggplants (2-lbs., 0.9-kg.)

The Spices
- Olive oil – ¼ cup
- Balsamic vinegar – ¼ cup
- Minced garlic – 2 tablespoons
- Salt – ½ tablespoon
- Pepper – ½ teaspoon

The Liquid
- Water – 2 cups

The Heat
- Maple wood chips, soak for an hour

Method
1. Pour water into an iron pan then place in the gas smoker.
2. Add the soaked wood chips to the tray and set it in the gas smoker.
3. Ignite your gas smoker and get it ready. Let it reach 200°F (93°C).
4. Add balsamic vinegar, minced garlic, salt, and pepper to the olive oil then stir well.
5. Cut the eggplants into halves lengthwise then place in the gas smoker.
6. Drizzle the spice mixture over the halved eggplants then smoke for approximately 45 minutes or until cooked through.
7. Once it is done, remove the smoked eggplants from the gas smoker and transfer to a serving dish.
8. Serve and enjoy.

(Cooking Time 2 Hours 10 Minutes)
Ingredients for 10 servings
- Pumpkin (5-lb., 2.3-kg.)

The Glaze
- Olive oil – 3 tablespoons
- Maple syrup – 3 tablespoons
- Salt – ½ teaspoon
- Pepper – ½ teaspoon

The Liquid
- Water – 2 cups

The Heat
- Maple wood chips, soak for an hour

Method
1. Pour olive oil and maple syrup into a bowl then stir until incorporated.
2. Season with salt and pepper then mix well. Set aside.
3. Pour water into an iron pan then place in the gas smoker.
4. Add the soaked wood chips to the tray and set it in the gas smoker.
5. Ignite your gas smoker and get it ready. Let it reach 250°F (121°C).
6. Once the gas smoker is ready, cut the pumpkin into halves and place in the gas smoker.
7. Smoke the pumpkin for approximately 2 hours and baste the maple syrup mixture once every 20 minutes.
8. Wait until the pumpkin is tender then remove from the gas smoker.
9. Baste the remaining maple syrup mixture over the smoked pumpkin then serve.
10. Enjoy!

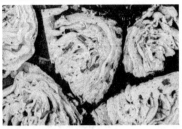

(Cooking Time 1 Hour 5 Minutes)

Ingredients for 10 servings

- Cabbage (2-lbs., 0.9-kg.)

The Glaze

- Butter – ¼ cup
- Honey – 3 tablespoons
- Salt – ½ teaspoon
- Pepper – ½ teaspoon
- Brown sugar – 1 ½ tablespoons
- Garlic powder – 1 teaspoon
- Onion powder – 1 teaspoon

The Liquid

- Water – 2 cups

The Heat

- Apple wood chips, soak for an hour

Method

1. Place butter in a saucepan and preheat over low heat.
2. Once the butter is melted, add salt, pepper, brown sugar, garlic powder, and onion powder to the saucepan. Stir until dissolved and remove from heat.
3. Drizzle honey over the melted butter then stir well. Set aside.
4. Next, pour water into an iron pan then place in the gas smoker.
5. Add the soaked wood chips to the tray and set it in the gas smoker.
6. Ignite your gas smoker and get it ready. Let it reach 250°F (121°C).
7. When the gas smoker is ready, cut the cabbage into wedges then place in the smoker.
8. Baste the cabbage wedges with the honey mixture then smoke for approximately an hour or until tender.
9. Flip the cabbage wedges once every 15 minutes and baste the remaining honey mixture over the cabbage.
10. Once the smoked cabbage is tender, remove from the gas smoker and transfer to a serving dish.
11. Serve and enjoy.

CHAPTER-9 INFORMATION ON SMOKING MEAT

Gas Smokers

Using Gas Smoker will allow you to enjoy a wide variety of recipes that range of smoked meats, veggies and different types of ingredients that you can cook both indoors and outdoors alike. And not only gas smoker is easy to use, but it needs a very minimal effort to get your dishes ready. And what is great about gas smoker is that it can offer you the same delicious taste conventional wood smokers grant you. In general, the temperatures of smokehouses vary from about 109°F to approximately 160° F. And usually, the whole process of smoking food takes a few hours to a few days to be perfectly smoked depending on the type of the used ingredients and meat. Usually, after the process of smoking food, the meat has to be rapidly chilled and cut; then wrapped to be prepared for retail and trading.

Gas Smoker Benefits

Gas fuelled smokers are known for having many benefits and great qualities and unlike conventional smokers, gas smokers are known for their efficiency and for the versatility of this type of cookware. And here some of the most important advantages of using a Gas smoker:

1.   Gas smokers can make smoking foods easier as you can use this type of smoker whatever weather whether in rainy or even windy weather without any risks. Besides, Gas smokers are safe to use by all people.

2.   Unlike wood smokers, Gas smokers are easy-to use while camping and wherever you want, even in places where there are no wood logs at all. And what makes lighting Gas smokers easier is that fuel is available wherever you go. Besides, gas is available in every location you go to.

3.   Gas smokers are known for its high ability to produce clean heat, which makes smoking with gas smokers healthier to use in comparison to conventional brands of smokers. And what is more exciting about Gas smokers is that you can still use your favourite wood chips like apple chips, chunks and hickory chips.

4.   Many gas smokers are equipped with a smoking cast iron box that you can use to keep the coals or wood insulated inside it and thus you can rest assured that your Gas smoker is safe to use and very easy to prevent chips from burning quickly.

Gas Smoker Safeguards

Gas smokers are characterised by the same design and simple structure as well as use. Gas smoker is connected to a propane tank or just a gas line and we can see this tank placed right onto the bottom. Gas smokers are also equipped with smaller lockers and you can a find a burner right into the bottom; the burner can be cast iron or brass. Above the burner of every Gas smoker; we can find a tight shelf designed to place a pan for the wood over it. And above this pan, we can find a shelf for water pot. And above this shelf, we can find four shelves for food ingredients. The bottom vents of Gas smokers can't be adjusted in order to make sure that gas gets the oxygen it needs to smoker food properly. At the top of every gas smoker, we can find a damper or two or a chimney. And to properly use the Gas Smoker, you should pay make sure to leave the top of the vent all the way open in order to prevent any soot from building up on top of the meat.

Basic tips that may help you master the use of this smoker perfectly :

1. **Season your smoker:**The process of seasoning your smoker is very simple and all you have to do to start is to coat the inside of your Gas smoker with the help of a film of smoke residue. And this step will help protect your smoker and helps keep it in a good condition.

2. **Carefully and gently wash the outside and inside** of the Gas Smoker with a small quantity of warm water and with a little bit of detergent. Then rinse the smoker with clean water and leave it to dry later.

3. **Fill the Wood chip box in your Gas smoker** with pre-soaked wood chips of your choice; then light your smoker and set the level of gas to medium.

4. **Be careful of using the water bowl**

5. **Once the Gas smoker is filled up with smoke**; leave your gas smoker to season for about 30 minutes. You can also re-season the Gas smoker from time to time and you can do this at least once per year.

6. **Before starting to use your Gas Smoker**, make sure to gather all the utensils and equipments for great results.

What is the primary difference between Barbequing a meat and smoking it?

You might not believe it, but there are still people who think that the process of Barbequing and Smoking are the same! So, this is something which you should know about before diving in deeper. So, whenever you are going to use a traditional BBQ grill, you always put your meat directly on top of the heat source for a brief amount of time which eventually cooks up the meal. Smoking, on the other hand, will require you to combine the heat from your grill as well as the smoke to infuse a delicious smoky texture and flavor to your meat. Smoking usually takes much longer than traditional barbecuing. In most cases, it takes a minimum of 2 hours and a temperature of 100 -120 degrees for the smoke to be properly infused into the meat.

Keep in mind that the time and temperature will obviously depend on the type of meat that you are using, and that is why it is suggested that you keep a meat thermometer handy to ensure that your meat is doing fine. Keep in mind that this method of barbecuing is also known as "Low and slow" smoking as well. With that cleared up, you should be aware that there are actually two different ways through which smoking is done.

The core difference between cold and hot smoking

Depending on the type of grill that you are using, you might be able to get the option to go for a Hot Smoking Method or a Cold Smoking One. The primary fact about these three different cooking techniques which you should keep in mind are as follows:

• **Hot Smoking:** In this technique, the food will use both the heat on your grill and the smoke to prepare your food. This method is most suitable for items such as chicken, lamb, brisket etc.

• **Cold Smoking:** In this method, you are going to smoke your meat at a very low temperature such as 30 degree Celsius, making sure that it doesn't come into the direct contact with the heat. This is mostly used as a means to preserve meat and extend their life on the shelf.

• **Roasting Smoke:** This is also known as Smoke Baking. This process is essentially a combined form of both roasting and baking and can be performed in any type of smoker with a capacity of reaching temperatures above 82 degree Celsius. By now you must be really curious to know about the different types of Smokers that are out there right? Well, in the next section I am exactly going to discuss that!

The different types of available Smokers

Essentially, what you should know is that right now in the market, you are going to get three different types of Smokers.

Charcoal Smoker

These types of smokers are hands down the best one for infusing the perfect Smoky flavor to your meat. But be warned, though, that these smokers are a little bit difficult to master as the method of regulating temperature is a little bit difficult when compared to normal Gas or Electric smokers.

Electric Smoker

After the charcoal smoker, next comes perhaps the simpler option, Electric Smokers. These are easy to use and plug and play type. All you need to do is just plug in, set the temperature and go about your daily life. The smoker will do the rest. However, keep in mind that the finishing smoky flavor won't be as intense as the Charcoal one.

Gas Smokers

Finally, comes the Gas Smokers. These have a fairly easy mechanism for temperature control and are powered usually by LP Gas. The drawback of these Smokers is that you are going to have to keep checking up on your Smoker every now and then to ensure that it has not run out of Gas. Now, these have been further dissected into different styles of the smoker. Each of which is preferred by Smokers of different experiences.

The different styles of smokers

The different styles of Smokers are essentially divided into the following.

Vertical (Bullet Style Using Charcoal)

These are usually low-cost solutions and are perfect for first-time smokers.

Vertical (Cabinet Style)

These Smokers come with a square shaped design with cabinets and drawers/trays for easy accessibility. These cookers also come with a water tray and a designated wood chips box as well.

Offset

These type of smokers have dedicated fireboxes that are attached to the side of the main grill. The smoke and heat required for these are generated from the firebox itself which is then passed through the main chamber and out through a nicely placed chimney.

Kamado Joe

And finally, we have the Kamado Joe which is ceramic smokers are largely regarded as being the "Jack Of All Trades".

These smokers can be used as low and slow smokers, grills, hi or low-temperature ovens and so on. They have a very thick ceramic wall which allows it to hold heat better than any other type of smoker out there, requiring only a little amount of charcoal. These are easy to use with better insulation and are more efficient when it comes to fuel control.

With the smokers now set up, the next step is to understand about the woods used in the smoker. Below is a table which discusses most of the general types of woods that are used in Smokers and their potential benefits.

The different types of wood and their benefits

The Different Types Of Wood	Suitable For
Hickory	Wild game, chicken, pork, cheeses, beef
Pecan	Chicken, pork, lamb, cheeses, fish.
Mesquite	Beef and vegetables
Alder	Swordfish, Salmon, Sturgeon and other types of fishes. Works well with pork and chicken too.
Oak	Beef or briskets
Maple	Vegetable, ham or poultry
Cherry	Game birds, poultry or pork
Apple	Game birds, poultry, beef
Peach	Game birds, poultry or pork
Grape Vines	Beef, chicken or turkey
Wine Barrel Chips	Turkey, beef, chicken or cheeses
Seaweed	Lobster, mussels, crab, shrimp etc.
Herbs or Spices such as rosemary, bay leaves, mint, lemon peels, whole nutmeg etc.	Good for cheeses or vegetables and a small collection of light meats such as fillets or fish steaks.

The basic preparations

- Always be prepared to spend the whole day and take as much time as possible to smoke your meat for maximum effect.

- Make sure to obtain the perfect Ribs/Meat for the meal which you are trying to smoke. Do a little bit of research if you need.

- I have already added a list of woods in this book, consult to that list and choose the perfect wood for your meal.

- Make sure to prepare the marinade for each of the meals properly. A great deal of the flavor comes from the rubbing.
- Keep a meat thermometer handy to get the internal temperature when needed.
- Use mittens or tongs to keep yourself safe

- Refrain yourself from using charcoal infused alongside starter fluid as it might bring a very unpleasant odor to your food

- Always make sure to start off with a small amount of wood and keep adding them as you cook.

- Don't be afraid to experiment with different types of wood for newer flavor and experiences.

- Always keep a notebook near you and note jot down whatever you are doing or learning and use them during the future session. This will help you to evolve and move forward.

The core elements of smoking!

Smoking is a very indirect method of cooking that relies on a number of different factors to give you the most perfectly cooked meal that you are looking for. Each of these components is very important to the whole process as they all work together to create the meal of your dreams.

- **Time**: Unlike grilling or even Barbequing, smoking takes a really long time and requires a whole lot of patience. It takes time for the smoky flavor to slowly get infused into the meats. Jus to bring things into comparison, it takes an about 8 minutes to fully cook a steak through direct heating, while smoking (indirect heating) will take around 35-40 minutes.

- **Temperature:** When it comes to smoking, the temperature is affected by a lot of different factors that are not only limited to the wind, cold air temperatures but also the cooking wood's dryness. Some smokers work best with large fires that are controlled by the draw of a chimney and restricted airflow through the various vents of the cooking chamber and firebox. While other smokers tend to require smaller fire with fewer coals as well as a completely different combination of the vent and draw controls. However, most smokers are designed to work at temperatures as low as 180 degrees Fahrenheit to as high as 300 degrees Fahrenheit. But the recommend temperature usually falls between 250 degrees Fahrenheit and 275 degrees Fahrenheit.

- **Airflow:** The level of air to which the fire is exposed to greatly determines how your fire will burn and how quickly it will burn the fuel. For instance, if you restrict air flow into the firebox by closing up the available vents, then the fire will burn at a low temperature and vice versa. Typically in smokers, after lighting up the fire, the vents are opened to allow for maximum air flow and is then adjusted throughout the cooking process to make sure that optimum flame is achieved.

- **Insulation:** Insulation is also very important when it comes to smokers as it helps to easily manage the cooking process throughout the whole cooking session. A good insulation allows smokers to efficiently reach the desired temperature instead of waiting for hours upon hours!

CPSIA information can be obtained
at www.ICGtesting.com
Printed in the USA
BVHW011127040421
604163BV00003B/258